T0083466

Within the Sweet Noise of Life

THE ITALIAN LIST

Within the Sweet Noise of Life

Selected Poetry

SANDRO PENNA

TRANSLATED BY ALEXANDER BOOTH

LONDON NEW YORK CALCUTTA

SERIES EDITOR
Alberto Toscano

Seagull Books, 2021

Italian original © 2017 Mondadori Libri S.p.A., Milano

English translation © Alexander Booth, 2021

ISBN   978 0 8574 2 787 8

British Library Cataloguing-in-Publication Data
A catalogue record for this book is available from the British Library

Typeset by Seagull Books, Calcutta, India
Printed and bound by Versa Press, East Peoria, Illinois, USA

Contents

From **Appendix** to *Poesie* 1927–1938

From *Poesie* 1938–1955

Life . . . is to remember waking
Sad in a train at dawn: having seen
The uncertain light outside: having felt
In your broken body the virgin
Stinging melancholy of the bitter air

But to remember the sudden
Release is sweeter: close to me
A young sailor: the blue
And white of his uniform, and beyond
A crisp and colourful sea

Autumn

The wind left you a clear echo,
In the senses, of the things you'd seen
—confused—the day. When sleep arrives
How defend yourself: a chrysanthemum
A trembling lake and narrow string
Yellow-green trees beneath the sun

If the summer night surrenders
A little at the sea-edge men appear
—born in silence like its colours—
Light-hearted and bare, then leave

But as the wind moves the sea, so
The men, shouting, move their boats

On their last sweat the sun

If behind the window's glow
A small boy sleeps, in summer night,
And dreams . . .
                    Quickly a train
Goes by, and far
                    The sea is as before

The sea is completely blue
The sea is completely calm
Inside the heart almost a scream
Of joy. And all is completely calm

Country Cemetery

Between the crickets' joy
Obscure flickers

And high above the stars

In that young
Heart the quiet whirl
Of daylight's
Sunny deeds

But an unease now
Spooks the laughing eyes
Of the boy who's come
With me in joy

City

Bruised dawn, I have no god

Sleepy faces move through the streets
Buried beneath bundles of icy weeds
Vendors bark at the empty cold

I've seen more deeply coloured dawns
On seas, on places in the country—but so what

I lose myself in the love of those faces

School

On blue mornings
The crisp black rows
Of boarders. Bent
Then over books. Trees
In the window banners
Of a rural nostalgia

All wrapped up in wind you descend
The black stairs of my *taverna*
Your beautiful tousled hair
You wear over shining eyes
In one of my distant heavens

In the smoky *taverna*
Now the smell of the port and of wind
Free wind that sculpts the bodies
And quickens the white sailors' step

Beneath the April sky my peace
Is uncertain. As the wind wants
The greens whip. The waters are still
Asleep but with open eyes it seems

Boys run over the fields, and
Appear riven by the wind. But really
It's only my heart: a vivid flash
(O youth) of their white shirts
Stamped out on the grass

On the slow cart a man's asleep. It's June
And the soul stirs with a vague
Certainty. O still skies. And naked bodies

But the boys' lively back-and-forth
Won't stop beneath the sun . . . Later, ancient
Night will bend them low with love

Immobile in the sky the stars
Summer hour the same as another
But the young boy who's walking ahead of you
If you don't call . . .

Already autumn speaks. At the dark
Windowsill, silent, I listen to my thoughts
Bend beneath the west wind roaring
Through the leaves of these my black
Trees that only come alive at night
Then I lock myself into bed. And am met
By a boy's song which pitiless night
Has brought: life doesn't change

I leave my job completely full
Of arid, empty words. But at the gate
The gods have put, what joy,
A boy at play with being bored

O desolate at dawn
Flight of lowly swallows
Above the deserted city

Amid spring's sweet
Dust, among sparkling cars
You'll return

When midnight comes you'll find
Men still clinging to their glasses and their friends
But reminded of tomorrow's dreams
With slow grace an adolescent face
Retreats

It was September. The streets
Once more were full of shouts. The sun
Loved wine and the worker. Songs
Burnt late into the night
                                But a young boy
Stayed behind, astonished, then bewitched
—in the sultry canopy of an evening—
By the innocent laugh of a friend

Lullabied I'd like to live
Within the sweet noise of life

Down into the station's cool pissoir
I've come from the glowing hill
The sweat and dust upon my skin
Delight me. The sun still sings within
My eyes. Now body and soul I abandon
Between the polished white porcelain

Little one don't run away, don't go
Away alone. I'm not telling you this for me
I saw a clear sign upon your forehead
Your mother doesn't see. Neither does your friend

The September moon above the dark valley
Lulls the farmers' song to sleep

An insistent rhythm: soft
The animal breath, in the silence
And if the moon rises the valley will sail

A different breath here, sweet animal
Also silent. But a surge of life in me
Repeats an ancient life

I'll never be more alive

When the light weeps across the streets
I long to squeeze a young boy, in silence, to me

The trains that once languished here
Are silent. My life, it's pointless
Your hunger stubborn. Alone
On the night-soaked road the worker
With his cough at the end of February

The river is deserted. And you know
That yesterday's sunny surrenders are gone
I kiss your armpits, humid, proud
Smells of a summer going wrong

When the sweet and clamorous dusk
Would sing across the city, blessed, ancient
Sluggish caravans would carry
The young workmen's grimy clothes away

Unknown to all (and how much more to himself!)
Among the smelly and sweaty clothes he loved to go
—in the delightful outskirts' drift—
An angel. (And believe me: not the one who writes today)

It wasn't the city where evenings
Intoxicated I sang among the scattered lights
Above the sweet, sultry river
Now a blond sun on the black
Shop of my father seems to burn
Our absence. And I can't find the river

With a flick of the wrist you freed
A lock of hair from your forehead
Proudly lit your cigarette
But the hair falls back. And the season
Lingers and languid laughs

Summer dawn arrives. O first light
On my brother's bed. In the silence
The still confusion: laundry and sex
When summer comes leave this
Unhappy passion. In the silence
You reach the peaceful sea of light

Maybe simple poetry descends
Distracted like a traveller's hand
In the arid crowd of a train
Upon a young boy's back

The insomnia of swallows. The quiet
Friend at the station to greet me

It's sweet to cry when the sky is quiet
And water shimmers in the yards
Of youthful desperation

I loved everything in the world. And had nothing
But my empty notebook beneath the sun

Cemetery lights don't tell me
The summer night's not beautiful
And beautiful too the drinkers
In distant *osterie*

Like antique friezes
They move beneath the sky
New with stars

Cemetery lights, calm fingers
Count slow evenings. Don't tell me
The summer night's not beautiful

To sit at an unknown table
To sleep in someone else's bed
To feel the already empty square
Swell in a tender goodbye

It was my city, the empty one
At dawn, full with one of my desires
But my love song, my most honest one
To others remained unknown

Here's the young boy aquatic and happy
Here's the young boy pregnant with light
More limpid than the verse he recites
Sweet season of silence and sun
And this festival of words within me

Unexpected from out of the bushes, still
Partially nude, and disappeared at once
In that hour's heat a hot
Odour, some flies—and me with them

Late from a Sunday dance hall
The one o'clock bus blew down
With a streamer's joy and whisked him back
Home once more to his pillow

Train delayed at least an hour
The sea turns a darker blue
On the mortared wall the doorbell
Doesn't ring. The iron bench
Broils in the sun. The cicadas now
Sole masters of the hour

A dream of beauty one day took hold of me
Among warm people in a warm country

When the forms of the world would shimmer
In the soft October sun
Happy and harsh it was beautiful
To dream

And furthermore I'm alone
What remains: the sweet company
Of luminous, ingenuous lies

Drowsy autumn arrives. Sparkling
Behind shining glass two
Shining eyes

Claiming 'mother nature . . .' you, leaving
But what do women know about it, your beauty

Is the indecisiveness you hide maybe
Just a confused dream of the gods?

Here's the dear city where the dead
Of night doesn't frighten you. Lonely
Friends pass by with loving looks
Or at least that's what you think . . .

It's wonderful to work
In the dark of a room
One's mind on vacation
Along a sea of blue

Maybe youth is only this
Unending and guiltless love of the senses

'Then let me go if dawn's already here'
And so I found myself alone again
Among the empty and endless cabins by the sea
Among the mute and anonymous booths
Was I trying to find a home as well?
Hadn't the sea, the clear sea turned me away
With its light? Was only unhappiness left?
Dawn, tired, brought me back to a road

A thought of love returns
To the tired heart
As in winter twilight
A young boy
Homeward against the sun

The wind gives me peace and the rushing
Fountain oblivion. And in the meantime I'm thinking
About starting over. Paused in this piazza
Where the people pause around me

Deep in the night
The stars devour themselves
And a pain overwhelms me:
A love of beautiful things

Evening

To lose yourself in the fog. Quite far
From father and from brother
To lose yourself in these
Dear, dear faces. Hold
Within your heart the luminous eyes
Of that tiny face of coal

Tell me, veil-less light
Of the sky is this the way
You passed across his face?

Moralists

The world which to you seems made of chains
All of it is with the profoundest harmonies braid

O the rusty lament
Of too ancient a regret
From chimneys in the silence
Of night within the wind

On the grass maybe one morning

My secret story was born: improper loves

In a suburb on holiday

Silent rain from swollen clouds

City lights on the empty countryside

Watching a Young Boy Sleep

You're going to die, little one, and so will I
Still, even more beautiful boys than you
Will sleep in the sun by the seashore

And yet, we'll be nothing but ourselves again

Kiss me, end of summer, on the mouth
Tell me you won't go too far away
Come back with love upon your shoulders
And your weight won't have been in vain

Night, height of summer
Your windows full
Of family life. My silence
Amid dark leaves

At first breath of fall the train
Dear friend speaks of far away

'Escape' you say but why won't it rain
On the reapers barefoot along the hills?
Fountain sparkle at St Peter's—what escape
The Colosseum's just cowardly ruins

Goodbye, young one, go back into the dark
And this will be my way, dark along the river
As long as the world shall want it. But our secret
Light, from time to time, again will flame

Awash in light the bike awaits
The dishevelled boy without a voice

But absent from this dark dive
Full of smoke, full of words
I'm dreaming of a small village
Cemetery, quiet beneath the sun

Swaggering and gentle in Rome a flash
Virility pulses, laughs

Black fire between surf
Your eyes, confused, caught up in a dream
Of travel and solitude, you, my love

Furnished room in the *vicoletto*
Church bell there at the foot of the bed
Is love not a tight knot
Between angst and exultation?

The heat, the cold, of waiting rooms
The world it seemed to me a clear dream
Everyday life a legend

How beautiful the summer evening is
Chatting away in an outdoor cafe
Or better still the slow
Enchanted bliss: to listen
No disgrace at all in this

I'm always looking out of a window
So utterly in love with life
Fleeting and discreet the heavens' gift
To me—to join words to humankind

A crowd snarled 'to us' 'to us'
And black reigned beneath the sun
But the new urban planning!
The restlessness of the pissoirs!
And evenings the calm worry of cats

Maybe it's better to suffer than enjoy
Or maybe it's all the same. Snow
Is also more beautiful than sun. But as for love . . .

Sometimes, when walking
Down the street, next to a window
All aflame did it never occur to you
To speak a name, O night?
Only your silence responded
But the stars sparkled all the same
And my heart beat for me alone

Love appeared at a window and asked
Gentlemen, do you recognize my face?
They all said *yes* but the window
Had closed again. And love began
A game of affections that will end
Only when we are able to ascend
To that room and see who's there

The sun along the river was as innocent
As a sweet slacker's boredom
But at evening the dripping swimmer
Was still in the grey in which he spoke

I was going home. A stream of blood
Smirked in the dust of my face

Now I am not going home. In the dust
My soul's been trampled, and with it my smile

Literature

From the far side of the river a song
Drunk boys on a night in July
Dark, empty, I sat on the ground
Once upon a time I'd been Hölderlin . . . Rimbaud . . .

May now the time come
To buy what I can of beauty
Without a heart or high
Ideals. It's come to that

Another world is opening, a dream
My blessed girl beneath
The very sun (O the ancient
And gilded boys). A gentle dream
This life . . .
Remember me, god of love

At first cricket call, when the air is still
All light, I renounce the long
Arid list all these nightly trysts

Immobile and lost, in the dark
Slowly the hand awoke

Does beauty still exist in the world?
Oh I don't mean delicate lines
But at the station, brimming with intoxication
The young man, on distant shores his eyes

To Renzo Vespignani

Slowly nights ascended
And the world was blessed
My youth was the gentle
Gentle and sudden joy of a soldier

Then war came or, in life,
The nights no longer slowly ascended
Dusty the sunsets. And unending
Springs' heavy boredom

To Eugenio Montale

The frolic towards twilight I go
In the opposite direction of the crowd
Happily and quickly leaving the stadium
I look at no one and look at all
Now and then collect a smile
Rarer still a cheerful hello

And I no longer remember who I am
I'm sorry then to have to die
Dying seems too unfair
Even if I don't remember who I am

Translator's Acknowledgements

Grateful acknowledgement and thanks are due to the editors of the following journals in which many of these translations first appeared: *American Poets Abroad, FreeVerse, Italian Poetry Review, Journal of Italian Translation,* and *Poeti e Poesia,* and to the editors of the book *Next Stop: Italy.* In Rome, I would like to thank Peter Lerner for his close reading and detailed commentary on early drafts as well as for our many discussions back and forth across the *zona* over the years; Filippo Graziani, Francesco Graziosi, Craig Peritz, Valentina Stani, Nicholas Stanley-Price, Francesca Toticchi, and Paola del Zoppo; Archie Pavia at Libreria '900 di Carta; and Catia Gabrielli and Angelo at Libreria Fahrenheit 451. In Perugia, Marc Alan Di Martino. I would also like to extend a special note of thanks to the poet W. S. Di Piero, among the earliest of Sandro Penna's translators into English, and to Penna's friend and biographer Elio Pecora, for their encouragement.